Everyone
Has A Mountain

Beth Raynor Webb

ISBN:1515019551
ISBN-13: 978-1515019558

DEDICATION

This book is dedicated to our very first granddaughter, Brynn Louise, and to any other grandchildren to follow! Before we even knew you, before you even existed, you inspired us to change our lives to be the healthiest "Bestemor & Poppy" we could be.

CONTENTS

ACKNOWLEDGMENTS

We are two regular people with two parallel paths, side by side, but two different weight loss journeys. Every person who deals with weight issues deals with it in a personal way. No two coping mechanisms are exactly the same. No two losses are exactly the same. What you'll find in this book is not a "how to" or a "before and after" but a collection of experiences and observations in which you will hopefully gain insight into what a large weight loss journey looks like. My journey approach almost always involves a hardnosed disciplinarian route, which is often quite useful, but my husbands' approach is more often the humor and comic relief we also need along the way. Scattered through the pages, amongst my reflections, are quotes from Kevin that I hope make you laugh and lighten your spirit if you're struggling. Our main purpose and goal is to get you to believe what we have both learned to be true, that taking a journey to a healthy life is worth the effort.

Anyone who walks this weight loss path knows that they owe a debt of gratitude to many people along the way, or weigh, as the case may be. First and foremost I want to thank our extended family and co-workers who consistently encouraged and lifted us up with positivity when we felt like giving up. Much love and appreciation goes to our children for supporting (or at the very least tolerating) the changes we made in the fridge, the pantry, and the family dinners! Thanks to my sister Erika for being my most enthusiastic cheerleader, even more than a thousand miles away. Lastly, an infinite amount of appreciation to Kevin, my partner on this weight loss travel expedition, as well as my partner in life. He inspired, motivated, understood, and had my back. His empathy and "get real" approach to weight loss is what kept me going. He never looked back, he never complained, and he never quit.

HOME SWEET HOME

I didn't feel like walking tonight but there is something about my "mountain" that beckons me at the end of a long, stressful day. I am tired but the sun is shining and I know once I get to the top of the driveway the breeze will be blowing and my thoughts will drift from the hectic office into the peaceful nature that surrounds my home. I step out, breath in the country air, and take my first step. It always starts with a first step. It is exactly two miles from my front door to the big red stop sign at the bottom of our gravel road. Those two miles are a descending horse shoe shape, making way around what I've dubbed "Hawk Ridge." It's not technically a mountain I suppose, but when you are at the bottom, and have a steep, two mile return trip climb, it sure feels like a real mountain.

I've always been drawn to mountains. I spent my childhood summers playing in the Adirondacks.

Our most memorable family vacation was to the Rockies. The coolest plane ride I ever experienced was flying right past Rainier in the Cascades. I was obsessed with "The Waltons" and everything Blue Ridge. My favorite traditional music and tall tales and legends came from the Smokies and Catskills. It seemed fitting that when we made the decision to get out of suburbia and move to the country, we chose the beautiful Schoharie Valley and hills to settle in.

The Schoharie Valley is situated between the foot of the Adirondacks and the head of the Catskills, far west enough of the New York capital of Albany that our workdays commute consists of scenes of corn fields and dairy farms. It's not uncommon for us to slow down for a chicken literally crossing the road. At first, location may seem unconnected to weight loss, but my journey was more than a figurative journey. My quest to get healthy brought me to where I live now. This hill and valley region of upstate New York has become intertwined with my body, mind, and soul connection. The hard working farmers that produce the fruits, veggies, grains and dairies that fill me are my neighbors. On my walks I can reach out and touch the very corn I consume. I can stand by the fence and talk to the cows whose milk I'll have on my cereal tomorrow morning. It's spiritual, and it was lost to me while I was existing in the rat race of suburbia.

My grandfathers were dairy farmers. I grew up in the country. It made sense that when I was soul searching and getting back in touch with who I originally was, I would be drawn to this area that I've adopted as my own. I just never realized how much this place would affect my ability to maintain my new, healthy life. Not only do the locals feed me, but the hills, creeks, lakes, and trails have become my activity playground, and the nature and beauty refreshes and feeds my spirit on a daily basis. The day I watched a bald eagle soar and swoop to grab a fish and bring it back to his nest I cried, not just from the amazement, but from the realization that the old, overweight, unhealthy me would have missed that moment. That's what I call a "MOC" or, "moment of change," when you realize you have done something the old you wouldn't have done. It's life altering.

IN THE BIG INNING

Kevin Quote:
"How do I crack my kids up? I just sing "Fat Guy in a Little Coat" of course."

That's how my father would start stories, and I would laugh every time. Looking back at childhood is a perfect perspective to analyze food issues, however it's boring, and it's been done to death. We all know we learn what, and how, to eat through our developmental years.   Maybe it was the homemade chicken noodle soup that comforted us, maybe the pumpkin pie that became our symbol of family gatherings. Maybe we had to clear our plates before leaving the table or maybe it was all those starving children in third world, faraway lands haunting our conscience. Whatever your hang ups were, whatever mine was, bottom line, we all developed them.   They became our food vision, food pattern, food habit. How I materialized these habits into adolescence and adulthood is the foundation of why I was more than 100 pounds overweight by the time I surrendered.

We play the overweight person blame game. We blame our upbringing first and foremost, and then we move on to current conditions. It must be our spouses' fault, maybe our kids and all the treats they want stocked in the pantry. It must be our job, or the stress we are under. It's probably hormones and our inability to control chocolate cravings. It's those darn emotions, yes, that's it, and we must eat for whatever we are feeling. Does any of this sound familiar? These are the lies we tell ourselves. We could call them excuses but really they are outright lies. So now I am going to tell you the truth of why, and how, we get fat. Ready? It's a secret truth no one in the mental health or diet industry wants you to know. Once you know the truth I'm sure they will be out of jobs. The simple truth about overweight people is that we eat too much, and the too much we're eating is of the wrong foods.

Now that you know the truth, a simple course in nutrition and portion control should do the trick, right? There is a slice of truth in my sarcasm pie. Most of us DO need to relearn what is healthy and start using some common sense with what we put in our bodies, but this isn't Nutrition 101. The real truth is that weight gain, weight loss, and maintaining a healthy weight is a complex, multifaceted, difficult subject. This is about the journey, the process, and what is required to successfully lose hundreds of pounds for good. It's about my journey, my husband's journey, and how I hope this helps you on your journey.

ALL AMERICAN KIDS

Kevin Quote:
"I'm not sure why my parents wouldn't let me sign up for Pop Warner. I mean, they let me go out in the back yard and play "kill the guy with the ball" and that was way more dangerous."

We grew up on the outskirts of a small town, caught between the memories of the 1960's and 70's, and thrown into the 80's as the world started changing technologically. Our graduating class was the first in our district to be offered a class in computers, a newfangled idea for the masses. People my age remember simpler times, but we aren't afraid of buttons, gadgets that light up, or anything with a screen. We were the first generation of Saturday morning cartoon couch potatoes, the first generation with cable and remote controls, and the first with video games, CDs and home videos. We remember the stories about the Great Depression and WWII, but we certainly never lived it. We were raised with old fashioned, traditional values; however we lacked the strict implementation of said values of our parents. After all, they were making a better life for us, an easier life. They were making sure we had all the resources and opportunities they never had. These resources and opportunities included food. No longer did we need a separate milk man, or a butcher, or even a baker. We now had SUPER markets, with all their prepackaged and centrally located heavenly convenience. Lucky for us there were now preservatives to keep our food "fresh" and color dyes to make our food exciting. Why should we eat boring brown whole grains when we could eat sugary, colorful loops of sweet and crunchy happiness?

The good news is we also still rode our bikes around the neighborhood, climbed trees, and participated in rousing backyard games of baseball, football, tag, and kick the can. Everyone was always moving therefore those pixie sticks and bomb pops didn't catch up to us until later. The point of this walk down memory lane is to understand how food becomes part of our history, to see how food choices and patterns develop into habit, and aren't we all just creatures of habit?

Another habit I developed while growing up was

my husband. I married the boy down the road. It's the real deal, all American story of elementary playmate, middle school crush, high school sweetheart, engaged through college and then married with two kids. As late teens and into early twenty something, we gave the appearance of two healthy young adults. Truth is, by that point, we were pizza eating, desert craving machines. As the years started coming on, so did the pounds.

BETTER IS BETTER, RIGHT?

Kevin Quote:
"Geez, when we were kids our Cool Whip containers were filled with fire crackers and we just blew stuff up all the time."

Weight gain is sometimes sneaky. It happens when you aren't paying attention. It happens when you're too busy to notice, or too busy to care. It happens when everything is easy, everything is comfort oriented, everything is "better." While the hubby and I were continuing the tradition of making life "better" for our own children, we forgot the food to body connection. Yes, our bodies were made to consume food, but we were not made to be consumed by food. Until we made that connection, until we figured out that what we put in our body is for fuel, we wouldn't make the changes necessary for a healthy lifestyle. When it's all about emotion, comfort, or convenience, it can't be about health, and it certainly can't be about a healthy weight.

So there we were, a young couple, just starting out, starting a family. What were the plans? What did we want for our journey in this life together? Certainly children were in the future. How about a house? Of course, let's buy a nice house, get into a nice neighborhood, a five star school district. We thought about a good family car, a good family pet, a good sports program, a good arts and music program. Nowhere in our plan was "get fat." Nowhere in our plan was "let our children eat junk." Life happens, and when you are focused on some areas, inevitably other areas fall along the wayside.

Fast forward a few decades. By some measure we succeeded with "better." Our son and daughter had an enormity of resources and opportunity we never had. They had lovely homes to live in and lovely cars to ride in. They could be, and were, involved in everything and anything they wanted to be involved in. Our garage was strewn with a plethora of sporting equipment, the best of the best. Our basement was a virtual music and art supply store, the best of the best. Great schools, colleges, churches, teams, bands, by all accounts we had done "better." All of the sudden we realized all our initial life plans were completed. Now what?

JUST THE TWO OF US

Kevin Quote:
"Did I tell you about the time I tumbled out of the golf cart but didn't spill one drop of my beer?"

When your youngest goes off to college there is a mixture of emotion. There is a quantity of reflection that only occurs in large milestones of life. There is also the rediscovering of date night. We can go to any restaurant we want, as often as we want. There is no need for a council meeting to come to a consensus on what toppings are acceptable on the pizza order. Wine pours openly at dinner and cooking for two becomes a delightful culinary obsession. Empty nests are a blast. Doctor visits, not so much.

The first "sign of the times" began with high cholesterol readings for Kevin. "Here, take this pill and your cholesterol will go down, and by the way, you should really drop a few pounds." Thanks Doc. I had heard the stories about some negative side effects of these medications. I wasn't too thrilled that my husband now needed medications. By this point we were both morbidly obese, but we were content, comfortable, and really didn't care much. A pill a day was the first crack in our "better" life. Time elapsed and then there were some blood sugar issues. Kevin would get dizzy if he hadn't eaten. Our lust for fatty, salty, sugary foods had us on a path of deterioration. I was experiencing acid reflux and started taking a prescription for that. We both had back issues, ruptured and bulging discs which lead to surgeries. We both had knee issues. Then the mention of blood pressure medication came for Kevin. That's when a switch flipped in my brain.

It was a perfect storm of events. The health issues, the possibility of yet another prescription, our son's engagement, our daughter's upcoming college graduation, all leading up to my 45th birthday. It got me contemplating the future. There would have to be a second act to our life play, and this could go a couple different ways.

In my mind's eye I could see one path where we would celebrate showers, weddings, graduations, even grandbabies. We would happily pose for pictures with our loved ones at these events. On the second path I was a bystander. These events would still take place, but I would hide in the background, watch but not participate, and in the darkest recesses of my thoughts, I might be there alone. I looked at my big teddy bear of a husband, knowing full well what happens to men his age, at his weight, in a stressful job, on medications. A young widow was not "better."

AND SO IT BEGINS

Kevin Quote:
"I like to put my blinker on AFTER the lane change just in case they missed my sweet move."

"That's it. This is ridiculous. We are completely out of control, and if we want to be around to play with grandkids we've got to get our act together. Will you join Weight Watchers with me?" His response was quick and to the point. "Sure." And so in despair we found a local meeting and two days after my 45th birthday, on April 16 2012, we took the first steps on this part of our journey. Our tails were between our legs, our heads were hanging low, and our emotions were swirling. It felt as though I was committing myself to some sort of institution where I no longer had any say or freedom. It was something I had to do, and nothing that I wanted to do. Could we do it? And what exactly was it we were doing? The plan was go in, sit down, keep my mouth shut, and do whatever they told me to do and maybe, just maybe, I could lose a few pounds and not be quite so fat anymore. If I could just get to this weight or that weight, or this size or that size, that would be fine. If I could just stick it out long enough so my husband could lose enough weight to not drop dead of a heart attack. That's really what I was thinking. I had no delusions of health nut, or active, or normal size person grandeur. I was looking for just good enough to not die.

First meeting went well enough. I was able to blend in and I was grateful for Kevin being there with me. I absorbed what information I could, took home my paperwork, and got started figuring out on line tools and smart phone apps. If I was going to do this I was full in, still unconvinced that it would actually work. I remember the fear going back to my second meeting, having no clue if it worked. I never weighed myself at home so I had no idea if it was working. Low and behold it was, and I was on my way. So was Kevin.

The weeks and months became somewhat of a blur of highs and lows. I never had huge ups or downs. I had consistent, small loses. There was a range of emotions. I felt relief, excitement, anger, frustration, and hope, yes, mostly hope. With a few weeks of successful weigh in's under my belt, I became fear filled to switch anything up. In the early stages of the journey I ate almost exactly the same foods every day with very little variation. If it wasn't broke I wasn't fixing it. I was also mortified to eat anything extra. I mentioned that once in a meeting and people looked at me like I had two heads. This was an example of my lack of faith in those beginning stages. It was almost comical how differently Kevin and I approached the program. He certainly ate his extra treats! I was steadfast with my tracking, the one time in my life when being a tad obsessive compulsive has come in handy. Tracking makes one accountable. In our relationship I bore the full responsibility of figuring out the food values and tracking. If I didn't do it, it wouldn't get done. That initially made me snarky with Kevin, and I could have easily become resentful, but reality is we both had strengths and weaknesses on this plan and there were plenty of other areas where he was stronger than me, so I let go of snarky and instead embraced gratitude that tracking was an ability I brought to the literal table.

CH-CH-CH CHANGES

Kevin Quote:
"But don't those veggie burgers taste like hockey pucks? Pretty sure the guys at work said so."

Tracking what we ate was a major change, but not the only change. We changed most the foods we ate, the quantity we ate, the quality of food we ate. We changed how we shopped at the grocery store, how we stocked our refrigerator and pantry, and how we ordered at restaurants. We changed our entire relationship with food, started looking at it as physical nourishment instead of emotional comfort or fleshly gratification. Please don't misunderstand, we still love food and love to eat, it's just...well...different.

Movement became a constant in our lives. When the only "running" you've been doing for twenty years is in an SUV to sit and watch sporting events, recitals, and band performances, any kind of actual physical movement is change. We started by going out for walks after dinner instead of watching TV. Our short, slow walks grew into long, fast paced walks, and eventually became our first 5K with a group of coworkers. Our yearly trips up north to my grandmother's camp in the Adirondack Mountains no longer meant sitting in a folding chair watching others have fun. It now meant hiking, swimming, and kayaking. Changes here, changes there, life changes, journey changes, gradual, steady, permanent.

The movement change means more to me than any of the other changes. Movement means you are actively participating in your life. Movement confidence fosters relationship growth because through activity you build memories together. Think of it like a sporting event. Many people can be present at a hockey game. Some will be players, some coaches, referees, and some spectators. All are present, some are peripherally involved, but only the teammates will bond in relationship from their collective active participation. They appreciate those who came to watch. They rely on those semi involved like coaches and referees, but the joy in the relationship of teammates playing together can't be matched by anyone else in the rink. Move as a family. Move as best friends. Move as spouses. Move as coworkers. You will bond in ways you didn't know possible and make memories for a lifetime.

A friend once asked me if getting a gym membership would be a good start for her own weight loss journey. I challenged her with this response:

"Personally, I went to a gym for a while because our son worked there and could get us a family discount. It wasn't something I enjoyed and it wasn't something I kept up with so it never helped me much when I wanted to lose weight. It was one more thing I MADE myself do, like a punishment for being fat. So much of this is psychology. It wasn't until I found activities I LOVE, which really made me feel like myself and happy, that I was able to make movement truly integrated in my lifestyle. I thought about all the stuff I loved as a kid, as a teen. Activities like walks through the woods, skating, tennis, baseball, even gymnastics. Things I had let go of when I was older and overweight and just didn't think I could do again. I put all those things BACK in my life as my activity anchors. (Not all at once but as I built confidence) Challenge yourself to find movement you really love and then you won't stop moving. And trust me, I know plenty of people who go to the gym and they LOVE it and you might too...I'm just encouraging you to make sure you seek out movement you truly enjoy!"

I travel this journey with no gym membership, but I know plenty who do. It's about what works for you. It's about finding movement that you will continue for a lifetime. I know plenty of people who go to a gym regularly. They find support there. They challenge themselves there. They love how it makes them feel. I knew that wouldn't be me, but it might be you. For me it is the outdoors. Time spent outdoors makes the indoors seem vastly inferior to me! Winter, spring, summer and fall I find ways to move in nature. The unhealthy me wouldn't even put a coat on and go outside. Now I have gear for all seasons! You will find me trekking through trails, paddling lakes, balancing through high ropes courses, and even hooked to zip lines. I've decided my next attempt will be snowboarding. If you had told me a few years back that I'd be saying this, I would have laughed you out the door. Proof that this too, can be you!

Much of this journey felt like one of those scenes in a movie where you witness seasons in time lapse photography and pages of an old timey calendar are flipping translucent on the screen. You are aware that time is going by. You are aware that changes are taking place, but it's all happening so fast that there is no depth to the story line. Yet at the same time, everything feels like it's happening so slow it's excruciating. Once you catch on that it's actually going to work and you're actually going to get smaller and you've actually made changes to your life that are permanent, then it becomes a lesson in patience to let nature do its thing.

NOT TO GET ALL PREACHY
BUT...

Kevin Quote:
"She's not actually Irish if she doesn't like Guinness."

Maybe you are a spiritual person, maybe not. I consider myself a religious mutt, one who grew up in many different denominations of Protestantism, so to me it was always much more about relationship than any particular sect, or manmade label. Kevin grew up Catholic, bringing a whole set of behaviors and beliefs to our relationship that only a respectable Irish Catholic can understand. One might wonder what my faith has to do with my food, but it actually is connected in many solid and tangible ways. First, I remember being in Sunday school, probably around age five, singing loud and clear "My body is the temple of the Holy Spirit." That chorus still rings in my ears and for anyone who believes that we are to be the very best we can be physically because our bodies are hosts for part of the trinity, well, that's heavy stuff. Couple that with an overall general Catholic guilt that Kevin carries around, and one can understand how being morbidly obese and completely out of shape would be in direct contrast to what our faith charges us with. It may not have been the number one motivation that put us on a quest for health, but rest assured, it was always in our minds and hearts.

Secondly, as I began to look at food differently, I couldn't help but see the connection to Genesis 2:9 which says, "And out of the ground made the Lord God to grow every tree that is pleasant to the sight, and good for food; the tree of life also in the midst of the garden, and the tree of knowledge of good and evil." If food was not important to my God, He would not have made it a connection to both good and evil. I started pondering each food that I would consume. It became common sense to ask myself the following questions. Did this grow naturally from the ground? Was this alive? Is this good, meaning natural, as food? Was this put on the Earth specifically for my consumption? Is this food in its natural state? Meaning, does it have preservatives, dyes, and artificial ingredients? Will this benefit my physical body? These are seriously wise questions to ask yourself whether you are spiritual or not.

WHAT'S IN YOUR BACK PACK?

Kevin Quote:
"Hiking through the woods in winter was a lot easier when we had snow mobiles."

Like every good hiker, before a journey, one must take an inventory of what is in his or her back pack. Do you have what it takes to successfully get from point A to point B? What will you need along the way? What is essential? What is just in case of an emergency? What is a luxury item? It is the same with a weight loss journey. Some things are no brainers. For example, you must obtain a full understanding of nutrition and how your body breaks down what you consume each day. Without this you will wander aimlessly and fail to reach your goal. You must carry with you, at all times, the willingness to embrace change. If you are overweight, and you sincerely want to get healthy, something in your life must change. You can't expect to keep eating the same foods and get different results on your scale. Chances are MANY things in your life must change. Carrying that willingness will allow growth and long term success with becoming healthy.

If understanding and willingness are the essentials, then support and patience are next on the list. I am not oblivious to how fortunate I was to have a partner on this journey. Knowing someone else understands, knowing they will uplift you when you're frustrated, angry, or sad is invaluable. Getting a fist bump at a good weigh in, or getting a hug at a bad one, will significantly increase your chances for success. You may not have a spouse willing to join or attend weight loss support meetings with you, but there is no excuse for not packing your bag with support. Meetings are filled with people, just like you, who understand what you are going through. Reach out! There are friends, co-workers, and an entire on line community that you can access through computers, smart phones, and tablets. "I'm all by myself" is not an acceptable excuse on this journey, nor is it ever true. Ask the widow I met who has her grief support group cheering on her weight loss. Ask the single Moms I met who meet at the meetings each week and check in with each other on social media each day. Ask the college student I met who told me her roommate helps her plan meals and goes to the campus gym with her three times a week. These people filled their back packs with support!

How long will this journey take? Well, how long did it take you to become overweight? How long have you allowed yourself to stay overweight? How long is the rest of your life? That's how long it will take. The journey doesn't end with a time limit or a goal weight. It keeps going and going. Some sections of the path can be measured, but some can't. That's why carrying patience in your back pack will make your journey much more peaceful.

A NUMBERS GAME

Kevin Quote:
"If you don't know the caloric value I think it's like the metric system, ya just double it and add thirty."

We measure everything. We're constantly quantifying. We're obsessed with counting and calculating. There are pounds. What is your starting weight? What is your goal weight? How many pounds have you lost total? How many more do you have until goal? Measure your waist, your hips, your chest, you're your arms. Measure your food, measure your pants size, measure your dress size, and measure your BMI. And then there is time. How long will it take us to lose X amount of weight? I found myself looking at my weekly averages and looking at calendars and constantly calculating what weight I'd be at on what dates, and what size I'd be with X amount of pounds gone. I counted the costs as well. How many dollars will it cost? I legalistically gave myself limits. "I will not allow myself to go past the one year mark from when I started." With that quantified limit in mind I marched onward, week by week, weigh in by weigh in. My weight loss graph would look like a beautiful perfect line, gradually sloping downward from start to finish. I would be the first person ever to never have a gain on this journey, and for a good while, that held true. Unfortunately, as all perfectionists and control addicts learn, nothing is ever perfect and you can't always control everything.

One revelation on this journey was the need to strive for progress and positivity instead of perfection. Ouch. That's not okay for someone who doesn't handle mistakes or imperfections in herself well. Would I get angry at Kevin if he had a difficult week and didn't lose, or heaven forbid he gained? Of course I would not. Would I be mad at myself for the very same thing? Yes. My numbers needed to be perfect. Only a loss was acceptable in my mind. It's a dangerous result of over quantifying absolutely everything. Why is it dangerous? The answer is simple. Anything that sets us up for failure, including expectations of numbers perfection, will ultimately do a number on our psyche, and in turn, make our journey more difficult.

BOPPO THE CLOWN

Kevin Quote:
"I never torment myself at home. I only get on the scale at the meetings."

As a child I was given a "Boppo the Clown" blow up toy. It was a plastic punching bag with sand in the bottom that I stood eye to eye with at age three. When he was filled with all his glorious air and staring creepily at me, it was easy to let loose, haul off, and beat the nonsense out of him. It felt great to take all my fear, anger, sadness, any negative energy, out on this defenseless clown. The wonderful consequence of Boppo in my life was that I learned from a very young age to focus my frustration outward instead of inward. This is a lesson many people never learn. I know countless women, young and old, who beat themselves up inwardly on a daily basis. Kevin assures me men do too. Consistent inward beatings lead to insecurity, self-loathing, and often an inability to have a successful weight loss journey.

I'm begging all of you to stop. Stop picking apart your body, your intelligence, and your character. Your inner thoughts are powerful medicines or poisons. Choose the medicinal thoughts instead of the poisonous thoughts. On Thursday your weight won't be significantly different than Wednesday, however, on Thursday you can think positive, focus on your awesome calves, and be content, where on Wednesday you can think about how much you hate your fat arms, tell yourself you're ugly, and be miserable. Thursday is a good day. Wednesday is a bad day. Your weight situation is the same on both days, but your attitude made all the difference in the world. If you're mad about your arms, take it out on Boppo, not yourself. Find a literal punching bag. You won't be filling yourself with poison and you'll be getting some activity and toning those arms!

Be careful not to turn your loved ones into your Boppo. This journey is filled with some strong moments of anger. No one tells you when you begin there will be days you'll be bursting with rage that must be navigated through. There will be rage about a gain, rage at yourself for making a bad food choice, rage at the thin people around you, rage that it's taking longer than you planned, rage that it's costing you money, rage that you did everything right but the scale isn't showing it, rage that your sacrifices don't seem to be worth your results. My Kevin often became my Boppo, and for this I apologize. The good news is that the more you change, the more success you'll have, and the easier the journey becomes. The other good news is that for every moment of anger, there is also a moment of sheer joy. There is joy when you go down a size, joy when you fit into any chair you want to sit in, including a roller coaster seat or a plane seat, or a movie theater, etc. There is joy when you get a card from a coworker who tells you how much you've inspired them, joy when you reach an activity goal, joy when the doctor takes you off all medication, joy when you're told to line up for a family photo and you no longer worry that you'll look massive. Sometimes you'll just want to give Boppo a hug because this journey is so awesome.

WHEN THE LEVEE BREAKS

Kevin Quote:
"Wow, I haven't felt this dejected since I was 3 bills and couldn't fit on The Hulk coaster."

What I have learned from my own journey, Kevin's journey, and many other successful "losers," is that at some point, somewhere on this weight loss path, there will be a meltdown. There will be an emotional low point. There might even be more than one. Mine came June 2, 2013, the day after a big event that our weight loss group hosted. It was supposed to be an exciting day. Kevin and I had been asked by our leader to come speak at the event, share our story to help inspire others. I was already the weight loss "go to girl" whom my coworkers came to for support, guidance, and all their weight loss queries. My company lobby reception desk became a virtual confessional where people would come to recount their highest caloric sins and discretions. "Sure, I know how to do this. I can give a pep talk, get someone back on track, and remind them the journey is worth every difficult step. I got this. I'd be honored to speak."

As the event drew closer I began to feel an incredible pressure to be "done." My brain told me that I wasn't "done" unless I was at my goal weight. I wasn't quite there yet. I couldn't possibly be an example of success unless I was at goal weight. That's the poison I started telling myself. It didn't matter that I knew weight issues inside and out. It didn't matter that I had lost over a hundred pounds already. All my words of wisdom, neatly written on note cards, could not possibly hide the fact that I was a complete failure. Surely everyone in that room would see me as a fraud. It was past my one year anniversary point on the journey. In my quantifying brain that was the time limit I had given myself to be at goal. Since my start date anniversary had passed, I had obviously failed. Where was Boppo when I needed him? I went to the event, note cards in hand, feeling overwhelmingly unqualified, defeated, and like a complete hypocrite. I smiled and hoped that maybe the audience would be encouraged despite my unfinished weight loss performance. Now, here is a very important truth to understand. The poison I was telling myself was a complete lie. I could have chosen to focus on my positives and found joy in that moment of sharing, but instead I chose negativity, which led to insecurity, and stole my joy. I went home and figured I might as well quit this weight loss journey.

The next day happened to be our regular weigh in and meeting day. I didn't want to go but I knew I needed to force myself. I was sure the group would be disappointed with me. I was sure they were aware that I had failed. I was glad to walk in and see a big crowd, big enough for me to hide in. I made Kevin sit in the back with me. He knew how downhearted I was and has learned after decades together it's best to just let me work through such emotions quietly. I have no idea what the topic was that day. I only remember how raw I felt, how tired I was of feeling like I had to be perfect for everyone. I had to succeed for Kevin's health, for my leader, for the group's approval, for my coworkers' inspiration, it was all up to me. Don't let anyone down. In my mind I thought I already had. It must have been written on my face because as the meeting wrapped up, before I could slip away, the leader was right by me, asking if I was alright. My response was the most honest I had been since I had started the journey. No. I was not alright. I was an utter failure who had not met my goal in the time allotted in my head. I was exhausted from attempting weight loss perfection, whatever that was in my mind.

I call that meeting my second start date. It was my do-over, my Mulligan, my recommitment, and my journey freedom. There were no more set dates in my mind, no time limits until goal weight, no more self-judgment in the negative. I wasn't going to reach goal weight for Kevin, for my kids, or even for my friends and coworkers. This portion of the journey would be mine, and mine alone. The fact is this journey is never "done." There is no scale or measurement that can diminish what I have accomplished and I am more than qualified to share with others what I have learned. I am still learning. I am still making choices. I am still making changes. An ironic aspect to the event is that once in a while I still have people comment to me that they got something out of what I said that day. Even some leaders took away tidbits of weight loss insight that I shared. It is proof that we are never wholly aware of how we can reach and touch other peoples' lives in our personal journey.

FYI

Kevin Quote:
"When she told me I didn't HAVE to finish that, I informed her I NEVER leave food on the table!"

When you start shrinking, people notice. Responses vary. Fellow shrinkers encourage. All of the sudden you will hear "If I can do it, anyone can!" They tell you to keep going, don't give up, it will be worth it! Overweight friends become very nervous and sometimes try to sabotage. They do not want you to become someone new because misery loves company and change is scary. They don't want to lose "fat you" in their lives. Grabbing some fast food and drinks is too much fun to give up and "if you go all health nut on me you won't spend any time doing what I like to do anymore." They usually don't say that out loud but that's what it boils down to. I lost a few of those friends along the way. It doesn't make them bad people, and it doesn't mean they weren't really my friends, it just means they weren't ready or able to face something in their own lives that they saw happening in me. Most notably, people came out of the woodwork to contact me, talk to me about what I was doing and how I was doing it. It was a cavalcade of people who struggle with weight issues and wanted someone to talk to about it. People I never even could have imagined were struggling. People were so grateful that I was talking publicly about it and posting about this journey on social media sites. Everyone shared advice, recipes, and experiences. I received messages from older people, teens, men, women, high school buddies, family members, and some people I had never even met. What I took away most from the contact was that we are all in this together and everyone struggles to some degree with food, body issues, self-confidence. For all our differences, we really are the same. That's why "If I can do it anyone can!" is true.

I often try to soak in inspiration from my surroundings. It's impossible to attend group meetings without finding that inspiration often sitting in the seat right next to you. I've had the privilege of meeting some truly amazing people with some incredible weight loss journeys. This book would be incomplete if I didn't acknowledge the motivation they gave me and ask them to share some snippets of their journeys with you. It's important to note that every single one of these people have lost over a hundred pounds. This puts them all in a special club with unique perspective. They all know the struggles, the elations, and the requirements for the expedition.

Carolyn is a meeting leader that I first heard speak when she was substituting for our regular leader. Since then I've caught a few of her classes and also heard her share her journey at some special events. What makes Carolyn so special is not only the amount she has lost but how long she has kept it off. For many years she has stayed within her healthy range and that gives me an enormous amount of hope, optimism, and confidence that one can stay on this path forever. I asked Carolyn to share her thoughts on lifelong health.

Beth: Carolyn, could you share what maintenance and lifetime means on your journey?

Carolyn: I think I finally realize why it's called "Lifetime" membership. I have heard so many times "this needs to be a life style change" but never understood fully what that meant. The day I hit lifetime is where the real work began for me. This was the first time I realized dieting wasn't over because I was at my healthy weight. I continue to use maintenance to learn about my relationship with food. Our life changes, we go through different stages. I have discovered that we need to change our eating habits as well. I enjoy learning what tends to trip me up when it comes to food. I learned to laugh a little at the slips. I'm not a bad person because I just downed a bag of M&M's in response to a highly stressful situation. Everyone has those days. It is important to learn from this and move on. Goals are an important part of losing weight, but just as important during maintenance. We need to keep challenging ourselves. It is no longer about the number on the scale but trying new things to stay healthy. I no longer see a healthy lifestyle as being deprived. I have given myself an opportunity to live my life without being held back by my weight. That is so much more important than a bag of M&Ms.

Joe is a friend that I met at a speaking event. He's lost about 160 pounds and is still at it. I find his journey interesting because he brings a male perspective into an industry that is often marketed to women. We became social media friends and I noticed his posts were quite often about his workouts and about how he loves them and hates them at the same time. I asked Joe to give me his view on how movement and activity is part of his journey.

Beth: Joe, could you share a little bit about how movement and activity is part of your journey?

Joe: Being active has kept me motivated. Being

able to physically push myself outside of my comfort zone is extremely exhilarating! Only four short years ago I could barely walk a 5k, now I can run them without being too tired. There are days I skip working out. I, like many, have moments of laziness. I try to workout at least five days per week, even if it's just taking a walk or two. I have spent too many years on the sidelines of my life, now I'm in the game!

Kevin is the person literally sitting next to me at every single meeting I've gone to. He also brings a male perspective, but I believe his greatest strength is the laughter he brings to our weight loss journey. Humor is a large aspect of his approach so I asked him to reflect on it.

Beth: Kevin, could you explain the importance of humor on your weight loss journey?

Kevin: A good friend once told me "If you don't laugh you'll cry." I was known as the funny fat guy, often the brunt of my own jokes about being overweight. They say the best comics are incredibly insecure, and I believe it. It was easier for me to beat other people to the punch line when it came to making fun of my weight. I found humor was a way for me to get accepted when I didn't think my appearance would cut it. That could be considered sad I guess, but being able to laugh about myself has served me well on this weight loss journey. I love it when everyone is laughing in a meeting and it's even better when it's because of something I said. Anyone who is overweight understands self-deprecating humor, but the best part is when somewhere along the way I started talking about that person I used to be more than a hundred pounds ago, and it's at that moment I can really look back and laugh. A moment of humor in a very challenging journey is refreshing and needed.

EXCUSES, EXCUSES

Kevin Quote:
"Pregnancy weight gain? Tell me about it. I haven't been less than 200 pounds since before I had kids."

One of the most frustrating parts of my journey has been when people reach out to me, tell me how bad they want to lose weight, and then start the next sentence with "But I don't think I can because…" It's always, I don't have the money, or I don't have time for meetings, or I don't like to cook, or my kids won't eat that food, or my spouse won't like it, or I don't want to do it alone, etc. etc. etc. It infuriates me to hear these excuses. What people are REALLY saying is I don't want to use the money I spend on junk food to purchase healthy food, or I don't want to give up my TV time to go to a meeting, or I'm too lazy to feed my family the healthy things they should be eating and I don't want to hear them whine for the canned, boxed, processed crap they are used to getting. Ouch. I know I'm being rather harsh. I can say these things because those were my excuses too. Once I called myself out for the liar I was, I could start the journey. All I can do is urge people to get honest about why they haven't taken the first step yet. Remember, if you really want something, whether it's a material item, a relationship, or a healthy body, you'll find a way. If it's not important to you, I guarantee you'll find an excuse.

We also all tend to live in past moments instead of in the present when it comes to our weight. We know how much we weighed at different points in our life. What size were you in high school? How about college? Where were you right before you had kids or right after? Where were you comfortable? When were you comfortable? Were you EVER comfortable in your own skin? Have you struggled with weight your whole life or did weight creep up on you as you aged? We tend to drift back to glory days when we were younger and in better shape and we seriously convince ourselves that if we buckle down we'll be back to that fighting weight and shape in no time. We're under no pressure to do it NOW because eventually we'll do it, right? Maybe we'll start that tomorrow because tonight we have an event to go to. Maybe we'll start next month because there are too many holidays to enjoy this month. Maybe we'll start with the New Year or our birthday or the third Sunday after a blue moon after the first frost of the month? When will you start? Today, right now, is almost as good as yesterday.

WAIT, I'M NEVER DONE?

Kevin Quote:
"Oh I KNOW she's insane because then I heard her ask the surgeon how much does a gallbladder weigh?"

One of the coolest moments on my journey occurred on July 27, 2013. That day I reached my goal weight. Some people might look at that as the last step in the journey. It's not. It's simply one more reflection point. I allowed myself to stand still for a moment that day. I already knew my next steps would be back on the path the next day, tracking again, planning healthy meals again, I'd be making healthy choices again. Those last few hurdles to get to that goal were riddled with grenades. It felt like every step of those particular last ten pounds presented a challenge. That month we closed on a new house, moved over a period of three weeks, threw an engagement party for our son and daughter in law, threw a party for our daughter's college graduation, and then I ended up in the hospital!

It was a Wednesday evening. All the kids were visiting at the new house. We were all attending a company family picnic that Thursday but something didn't feel quite right. Buying a new house, the move, and getting ready for the parties had left me overwhelmed, stressed out and exhausted. I started having severe pain in my chest, had difficulty breathing, and felt sick to my stomach. The pain spread to my back. It felt as if someone was stabbing me with a butcher knife in between my shoulder blades. I knew panic attacks ran in my family and I assumed from the descriptions I had heard that this must be what was happening. I did my best to breathe through it. I'm tough. "Just calm down, you'll be fine. This is all in your head. You're letting your stress get to you. What the heck is the matter with you? I don't have time for anxiety attacks in my life." These were all the statements running through my brain as I distracted myself from the pain. I attempted sleep but it eluded me. Thursday morning I pulled myself together, put on a smile and went to work for a half day and then off to the company picnic. By that afternoon I felt the tightness in my chest starting again. I tried to put myself to bed when we got home but the pain kept me up again. Through the night it became unbearable. My body reacted to the pain with tears and vomiting. By five o'clock in the morning I begged Kevin to take me to the ER.

What I self-diagnosed as a panic attack was actually acute pancreatitis and I was told that if I had waited twelve more hours I would have been in the ICU. Twenty four more hours and I would have been dead. So much for toughing it out and breathing through the pain! I was on saline and antibiotic drips for five days until my enzyme levels were low enough to operate and remove my gall bladder. Lesson learned about listening to my body.

The next week brought recuperation, sleep, and then my first outing to a meeting. I was scared to death to find out what all those fluids and hospital food would do to the scale. I tentatively stepped up to see over a three pound loss. Phew. What I didn't count on was that next week, home alone, out of routine, out of work recovering with very little movement, and making up for an entire week of not eating! Luckily the scale was forgiving that following week and my goal of Lifetime membership was met. The hospital adventure of August 2013, as I like to refer to it now, taught me an amazing respect for routine and for staying on a tried and true path for success. It also taught me to forgive myself for such blips on the radar, because a bad week does not define me or my weight loss journey. It taught me I'm human. I'm strong but I'm also fragile. I'm able to have a stumble without completely wandering off the map. I might drop my back pack but I can pick it back up and continue the journey. That's what I did. Again, I got back to tracking and back to activity and making healthy choices.

Coincidentally, the week I reached Life Time Membership was also another week for sharing success stories. My leader asked me to speak again to the group. This time I did not have note cards, nor did I allow my fears or any negative thoughts to stop me. I shared what was in my heart about why I had joined and what this journey has meant to me. Two other members shared and I heard some comments that confirmed my suspicion that I was not alone in the struggle to take off those last few pounds. There is a complacency that occurs when you think you have reached the "good enough" mark in your own head. When you have a very large number to lose it's easier to handle when you break those steps up into smaller steps so it's not as daunting a task. It's a good strategy, as long as you don't allow yourself to except a lesser overall goal. I remember thinking on my first day, "If I could just lose fifty pounds that would be enough for me. I don't care that the chart says I should be down more than a hundred pounds!" That initially seemed unattainable to me. I had a certain number in my head that was "good enough" and once I got there I was going to march into my doctor's office and get a note that said I could stay at good enough. What actually happened was completely different.

About nine months into my journey I hit that initial self-proclaimed predetermined number. I knew I had a doctor's appointment coming up in about six weeks so I just kept tracking and losing for that time period. I'd give myself those six more weeks. By the time I got to the appointment I was already about fifteen pounds less than my predetermined number! My doctor looked at me and said I had been doing great but I was still a little bit on the heavy side and I should give myself more time and see if I could get down a bit more. I was so angry. How dare her call me "on the heavy side" but the truth was, she was right. My "good enough" wasn't really embracing a true healthy weight. So much of this journey is about facing the truth. I had to put my grown up girl pants on and come to grips with the true amount I needed to lose. Good news is, by that point, I already knew how to do it. Onward I'd march. My husband, my coworkers, my friends, they all kept me inspired on my journey at that point.

Fast forward quite a few more pounds and all of the sudden I found myself just a few pounds away from where the actual chart (and the doctor) wanted me to be. That's awesome, right? Well, it would be, except for the fact that I felt too fantastic! I was clothes shopping like crazy, having a blast trying on single digit sizes that I never thought were even possible. I was getting tons of compliments about how I looked and how far I had come and how inspirational I was. People assumed I was already at goal and when I told them I still had around ten to go they would make comments about getting too thin and becoming obsessed with getting too skinny. It's hard to stay motivated with those statements coming at you. Anger creeps in again. I was taken aback by how angry I got at that point. I felt like I had traveled far enough and had lost enough and these stupid last ten pounds must be some horrible joke invented to prevent anyone from ever reaching goal! This was just another example of me not wanting to be truthful. Again "good enough" was not really where I should be. I'm not done yet. Darn it.

So here's the truth about goal weight, reaching goal, and maintaining that goal. It's the real deal number. It's the actual healthy weight I should be. It's based on my height and my sex and whatever delusions I had in my head about where I thought I should be and where I feel comfortable and where I think I can maintain are irrelevant. What was in my head was based on all the baggage I brought to the journey. What's on the doctor's chart is based on what the medical community knows after years of research. Hmmm. I guess sometimes I'm wrong, darn it again. The good news is, once I accepted that truth and pushed on through to goal and beyond, I felt better than "good enough." I even felt better than fantastic. Absolutely nothing compares to the feeling that comes from being exactly in the medical healthy range, and realization you've learned how to eat for fuel and nutrition instead of emotions.

For Kevin, deciding on a goal weight came from a discussion with his doctor, not a chart. Again, another example of how different our journeys were. He lost and lost until his body naturally started maintaining. He maintained within a five pound range for over a year, and even though he was not where the BMI chart said, he talked to his doctor who confirmed what Kevin already knew. He was completely healthy maintaining right where he was. Goal weight and Lifetime membership achieved! There's not a wrong way to get there, there's just many ways to get there!

HULA HOOP QUEEN

Kevin Quote:
"I'm not kidding. It was a highly intense Badminton game. Oh the sweet sounds of shuttle cock."

Many years ago Kevin and I traveled to Colorado. Kevin had to attend a work conference so we decided to make a family vacation out of it. We wanted to have that quintessential Rocky Mountain experience but we were so large, and so out of shape, it was impossible to do what we wanted to do. We were too large to wear the life vests required to go white water rafting, and when we attempted horseback trail riding they had to bring out special horses that could handle our weight. It took extra help from the staff to get us up on the horses. It was so embarrassing we couldn't completely enjoy the experience.

You would think that would have been a turning point, but it wasn't. It wasn't until years later that we made changes, but these moments stick in you like super glue. I call these moments my "fat person scars." Moments when you must wait for the "special" seat on the amusement ride or when you have to ask for the seat belt extension on the airplane are public humiliations that send you longing for a magic pill and make you question your worth as a human being. There are levels of shame that one carries with every extra pound. There are certainly external disparaging overtones with being obese in our society. The fat jokes, and even the more subtle judgmental glances, all sting. None of that compares to the internal humiliation you afford yourself every day. I remember whole conversations in my head, yelling at myself, calling myself dreadful names when I would eat for emotional reasons. It's a vicious cycle, but it can stop if you make the choice to stop it. Now, every larger person I meet, I try to make eye contact. I try to send nonverbal wave lengths that say "I know, I understand, I have those scars too."

On the other side of being treated poorly as an obese person is being judged as a small person. Yes, the smaller I've become, the more I have noticed it and the more I'm in shock every time it happens. The shock stems from two different reasons. First, in my own mind I have never changed. When I was overweight I would forget that I looked overweight until reminded by society. Now that I'm smaller I forget that I'm not overweight. It takes a long time for our brains to catch up to where we actually are, and sometimes we never see ourselves exactly as we are. Secondly, being a person who has been every size from 6 to 24, I would never think to make a mean statement based on size so it always surprises me when others do.

My first encounter with a callous comment after weight loss was in Wal-Mart. I was feeling playful and I saw a box full of colorful, sparkly hula hoops. I couldn't resist. The sight of those hula hoops sent me back to my childhood summers filled with hours of fun, stress free activity. I was a hula hoop queen on the elementary circuit. I could keep one of those things spinning on me for hours! I wonder, is it possible? Could I attempt that again at my age? Could my new body do that old trick? Go for it! I picked out the blue one with silver glittery embellishments, and there in the middle of the toy aisle, I let my inner nine year old have complete freedom to enjoy that triumph! Just then, a rather large woman walked by and in a definite judgmental tone said, "We don't need to see your skinny ass showing off." I was stunned, first that she needed to make any comment, and secondly that she used the word skinny. My only response was, "Thanks, I haven't been considered skinny in a very long time." I continued to hula hoop until Kevin came around the corner, saw me, and we started cracking up. Let this be a lesson to all of us. We never know the journey another person has taken and we shouldn't use our own journey baggage to judge others. I wish I could walk around life wearing a T-Shirt that says "I lost over 100 pounds and I know how you feel." Maybe her interaction with me would have been different if she met me wearing that shirt.

EVERY DAY IS A WINDING ROAD

Kevin Quote:
"It was all a piece of cake after I shed that cake weight."

Sometimes the road is straight, sometimes it's very twisty. Every weight graph tells a story. Every person sitting in a meeting has a journey to share. Where are you? Are you at an exit, a rest stop, or have you gotten completely off the road? Are you out of control with no back pack in sight? Do you want to be on this journey? Do you long to feel "normal sized" or have you resigned yourself to walk a life path as an observer? Do you want to participate in your life? I'm here to tell you there is life beyond your couch. There is a place so much better than "just good enough" and it's not too late for you to get there. I will now throw at you the proverbial "If I can do it anyone can" speech that others gave me. Take the first step onto the on ramp. Make a decision, make a change. Oh, you've tried before and you've failed? How many times? Join the club.

I once visited a church where the pastor spent the entire sermon praising the people who only show up once in a while. He shared his love for the regular attendees. His congregation could not function without the steadfast, loyal, consistent flock. However; those people who come once, and then come back again months later, then maybe try it again the following year, also show perseverance. They demonstrate a longing, a desire to search for meaning. They could easily never return and no one would notice, but they feel a tug on their heart to reach deeper and ultimately they try again in order to add value to their lives. His point was "It's worth it." It's worth it to keep trying, searching, showing up and adding value. Each time you try you might learn one thing, one aspect that might help you the next time you try. If you keep trying, you will increase your chances that one of these times it will click! What if you never took the journey knowing that the very next time you tried would have been the time that you would have succeeded? No one can take the first step for you. It can be someone else's idea, just like it was my idea for Kevin to join with me, but ultimately he took the step just like I had to take the step. Let it be my idea. It's my idea that you fill a back pack with understanding, willingness to embrace change, support, and patience, and get on a path to health. I promise you won't walk alone if you reach out for a helping hand, but you must be the one to step and reach. Now go do.

But you're scared? Oh, really? Yes, I know fear. I know it well. Fear hangs out with insecurity like they are best friends. There were days I was so low in the pit that I was afraid to get out of bed in the morning. I was afraid I wouldn't be able to handle the day. I was afraid of people seeing me. I was afraid I was stupid. I was afraid of social events. I was afraid of judgment. I was afraid of failure. I was afraid of my past, present, and future. So I did nothing. I tried nothing. I was involved in nothing, not even my own life. I just observed others living.

It's about small steps at a time. My first hike was not a high peak in the Adirondacks, it was a flat, fifteen minute walk around my house. I let those tiny victories become stepping stones to keep trying new things. I let it ripple outward. I didn't learn to do things fearless, I learned to try regardless of fear! I've come to the realization that most of the time I'll be scared to death, but I'll do whatever I want to try anyway! It's freeing when fear doesn't matter anymore.

It's also freeing when you decide to let go of what

others might think about you. One of my favorite sayings is "The lion does not lose sleep over the opinion of sheep." This journey has taught me to sleep like a lion. I do not care what people think about what I eat, or how I look, or how I chose to be active. I don't care if I look stupid trying something new, and I don't care if I fail at something my first try. Fear and insecurity no longer hold any weight in my back pack. Let them go. Your load will be so much lighter.

THE SHAMROCK LEADER

Kevin Quote:
"A Job well done...well, it's done."

Some steps you take alone and they are for yourself. Other steps you take specifically to help others. Sometimes, those are the most rewarding steps. In October of 2013 I started taking steps to help others, first becoming a meeting receptionist, then leader certification, then personal coaching certification. The coaching calls I'd make, or the meetings that I'd lead, put me in direct contact to others going through this journey involving their relationships with food, but at the heart of it, it's about more than just food. I started using the shamrock as my symbol to help others visualize the aspects of the journey.

Think about how a shamrock is shaped. There are 3 distinct leaves but they are all part of one stem. I assign food to one leaf, activity to one leaf, and thoughts to one leaf. These are three very different areas, but all equal parts to the stem, or in this case, the weight loss journey. If we focus all our energy on one leaf, the other two will wither. For example, if I work out for five hours a day, but then go eat massive amounts of junk food, I will not be successful. If I eat the perfect amount of food calories but lay around all day, I may lose some weight, but I will not be strong and healthy. If I eat healthy and move, but constantly think negative thoughts and beat myself up, I will not be happy and balanced. All three leaves need attention, tending, choices and changes for growth and progress. I keep a shamrock in my mind's eye when I'm making decisions. "Does this choice foster growth in one of these areas?"

I also have a very specific motto for my meetings. It's "Be a participant in your life." I want my members to leave each week with a plan to somehow be more engaged, more fulfilled, in their own lives.

A LITTLE MORE FOOD FOR THOUGHT

Kevin Quote:
"Like Moses said to the shepherds, let's get the flock outta here."

Picture in your mind the healthiest person in the world. It can be a real person, a fictitious person, one you've conjured in your own imagination. What do they look like? How do they act? What do they eat? Are they on the cover of a fitness magazine or an L.L. Bean catalog? Are they an athlete or do they shop at organic farmer's markets? Are they super energetic and bubbly all the time? Whatever that person looks like to you, give that person a rating of ten.

Now picture the unhealthiest person in the world. What does that person look like? Do they constantly gorge themselves on junk food? Do they lie around all the time with no motivation? Are they out of shape with no strength? Are they sick? Do they complain and have excuses for everything? Whatever that unhealthy person looks like in your mind, give them a rating of one.

Look at the sliding scale between those two people. Now, ask yourself, what number on that scale is where you want to be? In all my days presenting this concept to people, almost no one tells me they want to get to a ten. I wonder why. Do we think we can't do it? Do we think it's unattainable? Do we think we're not worth being at ten? For whatever reason, I usually hear about a seven, eight, or nine. Okay, keep that goal number in your head.

Now picture a different sliding scale. On one side is the statement "I am willing to change everything." Give that a ten rating. On the other side is the statement "I am willing to change nothing." Give that a one rating. Now here's the tough question. Ask yourself where YOU are on that sliding scale right now. If you tell me you want to be a seven on the healthy scale but you also tell me you're willingness to change is at about a five, that gap of two is where the hard work exists. That's where it's not about the food, it's not about the activity, it's about the attitude. When you can get those numbers, where you want to be and what you're willing to change, lined up, that's when you'll be successful. Get that shovel out and dig deep. I promise it's worth it.

EPILOGUE

I didn't feel like walking tonight, but then again, I didn't feel like losing weight. And just like my weight loss journey, when this walk is done I'll be so glad I did it. It has been years since I stopped losing weight, and my body is content maintaining. My journey has continued. My challenges have continued, but my joys have multiplied. This health journey is so worth it! There is so much growth when we do things we don't feel like doing. There is so much to be learned outside our comfort zones. This is not just about weight. This is about change. This is about letting go of whatever excuses we use that prevent us from being the very best we can be. This is excepting that milestones are not beginnings or ends, they are just markers along the way. This is progress winning over perfection. This is about demanding more than existence from ourselves. It's about fully and whole heartedly living and loving life.

An after and before picture...I was always trying to hide behind my daughter in pictures. Now I don't hide.

The "best" before picture...because I was in my sister's kitchen, making an extremely unhealthy recipe, and wouldn't look at the camera. I did not want her to take my picture.

Kayaking is a lot more fun over a hundred pounds lighter.

The week in between both of us hitting our 100 pound loss.

A high peak in the Adirondacks is now common practice. Before our health journey we could barely walk up a flight of stairs.

Our 27th anniversary with both of us at goal weight!

ABOUT THE AUTHOR

Beth continues to live a healthy lifestyle with her childhood sweetheart Kevin in rural, upstate New York. She enjoys hiking, kayaking, and spending time with her dog, children and granddaughter. She is a weight loss leader and personal coach.

Made in the USA
Middletown, DE
16 May 2019